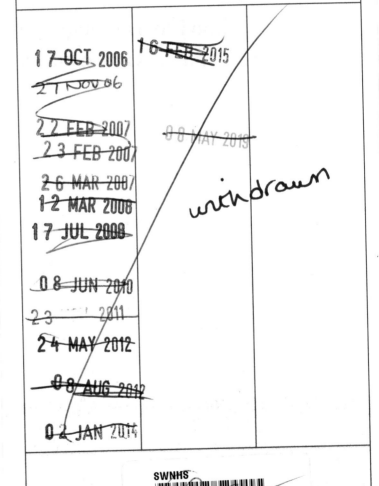

of related interest

Social Work and Dementia
Good Practice and Care Management
Margaret Anne Tibbs
Foreword by Murna Downs
ISBN 1 85302 904 1

The Simplicity of Dementia
A Guide for Family and Carers
Huub Buijssen
ISBN 1 84310 321 4

Including the Person with Dementia in Designing and Delivering Care
'I Need to Be Me!'
Elizabeth Barnett
Foreword by Mary Marshall
ISBN 1 85302 740 5

Perspectives on Rehabilitation and Dementia
Edited by Mary Marshall
ISBN 1 84310 286 2

Primary Care and Dementia
Steve Iliffe and Vari Drennan
Foreword by Murna Downs
Series: Bradford Dementia Group Good Practice Guides
ISBN 1 85302 997 1

Explorations in Dementia
Theoretical and Research Studies into the Experience
of Remediable and Enduring Cognitive Losses
Michael Bender
ISBN 1 84310 040 1

Dancing with Dementia
My Story of Living Positively with Dementia
Christine Bryden
ISBN 1 84310 332 X

The Perspectives of People with Dementia
Research Methods and Motivations
Edited by Heather Wilkinson
ISBN 1 84310 001 0

The Importance of Food and Mealtimes in Dementia Care

The Table is Set

Grethe Berg

Foreword by Aase-Marit Nygård

Jessica Kingsley Publishers
London and Philadelphia

First published in 2002 in Norwegian as *Til dekket bord*, by Nasjonalt kompetansesenter for aldersdemens ISBN: 82-91054-88-6

Copyright © Norwegian Centre for Dementia Research 2006

Foreword copyright © Aase-Marit Nygård 2006

Translated from Norwegian by Margoth Lindsey. Further linguistic adjustments by Alexander Mills and Jan Ivar Haugen

Library of Congress Cataloging in Publication Data
A CIP catalog record for this book is available from the Library of Congress

British Library Cataloguing in Publication Data
A CIP catalogue record for this book is available from the British Library

ISBN-13: 978 1 84310 435 3
ISBN-10: 1 84310 435 0

Printed and bound in Great Britain by
Athenaeum Press, Gateshead, Tyne and Wear

Mealtimes should be moments of enjoyment and company

Contents

Foreword

With a growing awareness of the importance of social relations for persons with dementia, we see how essential it is to make use of meeting places for contact and stimulation. Mealtimes are important events in the course of a day. Everybody has a relationship to food and mealtimes, to what tastes good and what is congenial. With a thorough organization of conditions the ability to eat on one's own can be maintained for a long time.

Mealtimes are more than food. They can imply companionship around a table with well-known activities, and can include possibilities of interaction and contact, positive experiences. In the monotonous days in an institution, mealtimes can constitute smaller or larger oases in the routine.

This book describes how mealtimes can become natural meeting places for meaningful activity between those who need help and those who offer help. We hope that many people are inspired by Grethe Berg's book and get an urge to make certain changes concerning mealtimes in the places where they work. Making mealtimes something to look forward to, or at least recognizing a laid table as something positive, can be a sound investment. The book gives numerous examples of how to plan and go ahead with a meal, so that both inmates and staff can experience the company as congenial and stimulating.

Aase-Marit Nygård
Oslo, November 2005
Norwegian Centre for Dementia Research

Preface

The subject of this book is how food and mealtimes can be used more consciously in the care of people with dementia. The book enjoyed success in Norway and a new edition was published in 2002. To my great pleasure a number of people have read it and given me feedback: they consider the contents to be a relevant description of practical experience, presenting daily problems in dementia care. I am excited and very pleased that an English translation of the book is now available.

I am confident that the subject of the book can be transferred across borders. In her book *Food Glorious Food: Perspectives on Food and Dementia*, Professor Mary Marshall of the Dementia Services Development Centre in Sterling has presented contributions from different countries on the same subject. My contact with her has been a great inspiration.

It remains a fact that the possibilities for medical treatment are limited for patients with dementia. The degree of success afforded by treatment still depends primarily on the measures taken in the environment and the nature of the care given to the individual patient. In our current contact with persons with dementia we see that the mastery of well-known, daily activities is of prime importance for well-being and quality of life. The things closest at hand matter most. That is why the book is as pertinent as ever.

The case studies are taken from my own practice as an occupational therapist in departments for people with dementia in the municipality of Ringsaker and at Sykehuset Innlandet HF, Sanderud. In these institutions I have had the privilege of facing a number of challenging tasks in co-operation with good workmates. The joy and inspiration that I have received from my work with both colleagues and patients and their next-of-kin has given me the energy and motivation to write.

My contact with representatives from The Norwegian Centre for Dementia Research has been of great value to me. It has given me professional support and confirmed my belief that I can make a contribution to better dementia care.

Arnfinn Eek and Eva Anfinnsen have also been available for advice and assistance in my work with the book.

Aase-Marit Nygård has been my indefatigable supervisor. She has helped me to concretize professional problems and to mobilize courage and abilities that I thought I lacked.

A great thank you to all my good helpers!

Grethe Berg
Brøttum, October 2005

Introduction

The aim of this book is to show how mealtimes can be incorporated into the treatment of people with dementia in nursing homes, sheltered housing and day centres. It is an invitation to dementia care workers to focus on the importance of mealtimes in care services. By planning and encouraging this social activity, the residents' well-being can be greatly enhanced. It is also a request to everybody who works with people who have dementia to participate in regular discussions about goals and daily routines concerning the residents.

The questions asked here are:

- How do we identify alternative ways of doing things?

- Why is it so difficult to transform ideals into practice?

The idea of writing about this theme is based on experience from working as an occupational therapist (OT) in a psychiatric nursing home for 25 residents with a dementia diagnosis. There I was fortunate to participate in a development project that was aiming to improve care and treatment of residents, increase knowledge and promote staff development (Lillesveen 1989).

One outcome of the project was increased awareness that mealtimes offered a means for developing care initiatives with residents.

After an assessment of residents in daily group socialization, we saw positive changes at mealtimes. Meals took place in a more relaxed atmosphere, with improved well-being and social interaction. Gradually, the staff regarded mealtimes as a high priority element in activities with the residents.

During my OT work in dementia care, I often find that the staff who are looking after residents are unaware of the practical consequences of dementia for the individual patient. They do not spend time systematically documenting their observations about the residents' abilities in daily life. This lack of record keeping leads to insufficient provision for individual care plans or subsequent use of evaluations.

The Norwegian White Paper No. 28, on the quality of care services (1999–2000), states the following: 'Correct diagnosis and evaluation of activity skills and resources form the basis for an improved quality of life among people with dementia disease' (Stortingsmelding 2000, p.52). This must be an aim for everyone who works with people with dementia. Staff responsible for the residents' daily care meet great challenges in using daily activities to survey the residents' resources and disabilities. This is fundamental as a basis for planning and creating care that can promote the well-being and confidence of the residents with dementia.

Mealtimes offer great opportunities for observation of levels of functioning. In this book, I will show, among other things, how we can use mealtimes as starting points for observation and surveys.

The book is divided into four chapters. Chapter 1 considers the social aspects of mealtimes and their significance to people's well-being and the feeling of being connected to others. Chapter 2 describes dementia, how the symptoms appear, identifying caring needs and which types of interventions have a positive effect. Chapter 3 considers meals in different types of residential care for older people and how they can be used as the focus of activity for residents with dementia. Chapter 4 considers conditions that influence our way of spending time with residents who have dementia.

In one ward the patients were divided into three groups according to abilities and needs. In the run up to Christmas it was the custom to go out for a special meal. In the group with the most seriously affected patients the staff decided to have the meal in the ward itself. The table was set with tablecloth, napkins, candles and Christmas flowers. Patients and staff were formally dressed. There was ample time set aside. The menu contained Christmas food that was easy to eat. They were served creamed rice porridge with sugar and cinnamon, chocolate pudding with vanilla sauce, caramel pudding with caramel sauce, ice cream and traditional Christmas cookies. The atmosphere was relaxed and non-stressful. The patients and staff thoroughly enjoyed the meal together. They had created a lovely 'out of the daily routine' experience in their familiar surroundings.

Mealtimes as the priority event in the daily routine

This section gives some guidelines for successful mealtimes.

The work in connection with mealtimes should be a priority for each day

It must be clear who is responsible for the planning of mealtimes, and who should share the mealtimes with the patients. There must be agreement in this forward planning and in how the mealtimes should be organized.

Staff should eat together with patients

Set the table for both staff and patients. Try to make mealtimes as normal and familiar as possible. Staff are models for the patients to look at as they eat. Think of yourself as a guide and a 'safety guard' during mealtimes. You do an important job when you influence mealtimes in such a way that patients enjoy their time at the dining table and eat well.

Help should be available when necessary

The person who is responsible for the meal must have the ability to assess the needs of the individual patient. Plan where staff and patients are going to sit at the table. Help those who need assistance. Let patients do as much for themselves as possible. The ratio of staff to patients should reflect the individual needs so that those who need help always have a staff member close by. This will optimize the patients' feeling of coping with the situation at the table.

Ensure there is sufficient time

We must know that we have enough time for our aims and needs during mealtimes. Dementia patients need more time to eat than other people. When staff are under pressure, this stress will be contagious, and this will cause increased confusion and restlessness among the patients. Dementia patients have problems dealing with several tasks simultaneously. Therefore it is important that we do one thing at a time. Give the patient enough time to put down his coffee cup before you ask him to pass the marmalade.

Proper equipment should be available

Make sure that utensils and food are ready for the mealtime. If possible, there should be extra napkins, cutlery and other things that may be needed at hand to avoid having to leave the table in the middle of a meal.

Ensure everyone is sitting comfortably

Make sure that the patients sit well and close enough to the table. Many need help to position their chair after sitting down. Patients with wheelchairs need help to adjust the seat and the back of their chair so that they sit properly at the table. Many sit leaning so far back in the wheelchair that swallowing can be difficult and hazardous.

The dining room should be quiet and orderly

Agree who should serve and who should sit with the patients. Switch off the television and radio. Close the dining room door. Put up a sign outside the door, so that there is minimal disturbance during mealtimes. Switch off the dishwasher and other kitchen machinery, so that noise is kept to a minimum. Be aware of how much and to whom you speak.

Ensure the lighting is adequate

Put on the room lights and table lights. Older people need more light than younger people do. Take care that the room lighting or natural lighting does not blind the patients. Many dementia patients do not acknowledge that too bright lighting has blinded them.

Make sure the food looks inviting and tasty

Set the table as you would for your own family at home. The food that is served should whet one's appetite.

The patients should be the focus of attention

The staff's attention must be concentrated on the patients. There should be a welcoming and caring attitude. The conversation at the table must include the patients and also promote a feeling of worthwhile contribution by everyone present.

CHAPTER 2

Dementia

Dementia is a common term for a series of organic diseases characterized by chronic and irreversible intellectual and mental deterioration. A
dementia disease also affects the emotional and voluntary functions
(Engedal and Haugen 1996). Dementia causes serious loss of self-care
skills and makes the affected person unable to control his or her own
life. People who suffer from a dementia illness are likely to become
largely dependent on other people for support and care. Investigations
have shown that more than 70 per cent of residents in Norwegian
nursing homes suffer from a dementia illness and that only 14 per cent
of the nursing home places are adapted for people with dementia (Eek
and Nygård 1999). This provides great challenges for the staff who are
responsible for the daily treatment and care of nursing home residents.
Managers who have responsibility for planning and organizing the
caring service in the municipality have an obligation to consider the
consequences of a dementia disease. The organizing of staff and residents and the provision of the proper physical surroundings and facilities are important. This will provide good care and effective arrange-
ments in order to maintain the remaining skills and resources of
residents suffering from dementia.

The following is a definition of dementia in old age:

> Dementia is an acquired organic brain disease affecting an elderly person. The disease affects the brain by loss of mental capacity and leads to weakness in the psychological processes such as speech, learning, memory and thinking. The disease is chronic, incurable, and deteriorates over time. (Engedal and Haugen 1996)

Loss of function and practical consequences for persons with a dementia illness

A dementia illness leads to serious loss of the ability to take care of oneself, generally speaking. Here we will consider some of the most common skills that are affected and the possible consequences for those who are affected.

Deteriorating memory and loss of ability to learn

Memory problems are an important sign of dementia.

> Petra constantly asked if anyone had seen her husband. She had forgotten the answer she received five minutes earlier, and that her husband had been dead for two years.

> Anna accused her fellow residents and the staff of stealing her bag. She forgot that she had put it under her pillow half an hour earlier.

Memory is a complicated function, and loss of memory can be seen in different ways. It is natural to consider that the ability to learn is connected with the person's memory. Memory is based on something we have learned. We cannot remember things we did not learn (Engedal and Haugen 1996).

Long-term and short-term memory

Memory is evaluated by using different criteria. A distinction is made between short- and long-term memory.

Short-term memory lasts up to a few minutes. It is connected to current activity, for example remembering a telephone number that one has just read in the telephone book, and then dialling it. To remember a person's name after having been introduced to a stranger is another example. Short-term memory can also be characterized as concentration.

Long-term memory is memory over minutes, hours, days and years. In psychology there is a division between three different types of long-term memory:

- *Episodic memory* is remembering specific incidents related to time and place. An example could be which clothing was worn on a very special day, such as a family anniversary celebration, or what a close friend or relative said on learning that President Kennedy had been shot.

- *Semantic memory* is the memory of factual knowledge, such as the name of the highest mountain in Norway, or the name of the prime minister of the country.

- *Procedural memory* occurs when one can rehearse a task that is performed automatically, without thinking about what one is doing. Examples of use of procedural memory could be cycling, washing hands, combing one's hair, eating with a knife and fork, or peeling potatoes.

Episodic and semantic memory are quickly impaired in residents with dementia of the Alzheimer's type, while procedural memory lasts longer (Engedal and Haugen 1996). This means that many residents with Alzheimer's disease can continue participating in practical activities that they have been accustomed to doing. This includes the daily tasks that have become more or less automatic, such as washing oneself, shaving, dressing, taking off shoes and tying shoelaces. Mealtimes and everything practical related to the intake of food provide possibilities for just the sort of activity that is automatic, for example buttering a slice of bread, pouring milk into a tea cup, and doing the dishes.

One of the nurses in the department suggested that we should bake doughnuts for Christmas. She took responsibility for the cooking of the cakes and organized the dough. Four ladies were placed around the table, each with their doughnut equipment. They all managed to make lovely cakes. It was obvious that they had considerable experience of baking.

Making doughnuts

Recollection and recognition

With dementia it is important to be aware of the difference between the two types of memory: recollection and recognition.

To recollect is to remember without any kind of help. For example remembering what was eaten for lunch the day before, which schools one attended, and the names of brothers or sisters.

To recognize is to remember with the help of a leading link. A sister's name is remembered after seeing a picture of her, or when we ask: 'Is your sister called Agnes or Annette?'

Irrespective of a person's age it is easier to recognize than to recollect. The difference in difficulty levels increases normally with increasing age. For elderly people with dementia the difference is even more marked than among healthy older people. This is an important point to consider when organizing treatment and care for people with dementia. The surroundings and contents of the residents' day ought to be influenced by familiar, recognizable and normal activities. Knowledge about memory loss provides us with a basis for caution when asking questions of residents whose memory loss disables them from giving an answer.

> Elsie wants to help making waffles. She has problems when we ask her about the ingredients, but she can confirm that the result will be even better if we put a dash of cream into the batter. She stirs in flour until she says the batter is right. She has no difficulties pouring batter into the baking iron or removing the waffles when they are done.

No problem getting the waffles off the iron

Prospective memory

Memory is not just remembering what has already happened, but also what will happen. *Prospective memory* or *planning memory* is remembering and maintaining future aims as well as remembering what is needed to reach this aim. For example to remember to keep a dental appointment in three days' time, to order the taxi, to check that one has money to pay the dentist and to reach the destination on time.

> Peter was asked to go to the kitchen and fetch the milk jug from the refrigerator. He returned to the sitting room with the newspaper. He had forgotten what he was asked to collect and returned with the item he guessed was the purpose of his errand.

This is a situation with which many of us can empathize. Most of us have experienced the deterioration in planning memory when we go to find something and forget what it is on the way. Shopping lists are a good way of helping the loss of planning memory.

> Johanna was encouraged to knit kitchen cloths for her grandchild, who had moved to a new home. She began to knit, but forgot what she was knitting and for whom. Motivation and initiative in relation to the knitting varied according to reminders from staff about who would enjoy receiving a gift from granny.

With dementia, the ability to remember what will happen weakens to the same extent as the ability to recall the past. People with dementia seldom do things on their own initiative. This may be related to the loss of ability to remember what has been planned and to maintain that. Without the possibility of being able to look forward to something with anticipation, motivation for doing things is impaired.

Loss of learning ability

As mentioned earlier, it is natural to see a link between the ability to learn and memory. With impaired memory, the ability to learn new things is limited. It is important to be aware of this when planning activities. In order to succeed in mastering a practical task, persons with dementia should start with the activities and equipment they know and with which they are familiar. To bake and prepare food, familiar kitchen gadgets should preferably be used. The whisk and the coffee percolator give older housewives with dementia a better chance to participate than if they are offered more sophisticated equipment. In the early stages of dementia, the first signs of disablement often appear as problems in learning to use new equipment, such as a new cooker, a washing machine or a microwave oven.

Loss of orientation skills

Orientation refers to how the person with dementia manages to remain aware of time, place, personal and family identity (Haugen *et al.* 1997).

Time

People with a dementia illness can lose the ability to know what time of day it is. Their internal clock ceases to function, and the person does not know if it is breakfast or dinner on the table. Some tend to reverse their sense of time, remaining awake at night and sleeping well into daytime.

> Sophie, who lives alone in sheltered housing, constantly telephones her son in the middle of the night and asks him to come and help her to change the light bulb, which has gone out. She has no idea that she is disturbing her son's night's sleep.

The relationship between past and current time is often disturbed, so that the person with dementia is more aware of past experiences than current events. The experience of time becomes dislocated.

> Although Johanna has been a pensioner for 15 years, she wants to leave the breakfast table to catch the bus for work.

> Lena is constantly worrying about her mother, who is alone at home and cannot look after the animals in the barn without her help. She lived with her mother until she died 20 years ago.

Place

Some people with dementia lose the ability to know where they are, and can get lost even in familiar surroundings.

Just before he was admitted to the nursing home, Anthony could not find his way home when he had been to the letterbox to collect the mail. He is constantly searching for his room and cannot explain where he is.

Personal identity and family

The ability to explain who one is, where one lives and to identify members of one's family can be impaired.

John, who is 87 years old, is a widower and has eight adult children. When we ask him to tell us about his family, he says that he has no children, and that his parents are alive. He can tell us his name and when he was born, but thinks he is 25 years old and that he is still living in his childhood home.

Linda, who was widowed three years ago, cannot explain when her husband died. She does not know what kind of profession he had, or his age when he passed away. When she talks about herself, it is difficult to know if the things she says are correct.

Intellectual decline

It becomes difficult to use information correctly. The person ceases to understand the practical meaning of the symbols on a sign, to make use of verbal explanations, or to understand instructions for practical tasks.

John can read the sign on the door which says toilet, but he walks past it and continues to search for the toilet. He is similarly helpless if anyone tells him that he should cross the corridor and pass two doors to reach the loo.

Pat, who has knitted socks for the whole family for many years, is no longer able to do it properly. There are mistakes both in the ribbing and also when she has to decrease stitches for the heel. Encouraging explanations or written instructions on how to proceed do not help.

Louise had difficulties in cooking the Christmas dinner. She could not remember how to organize it despite having done it successfully for more than 40 years. Her husband told her to find the instructions in the cookery book. Louise was still unable to proceed even after she had read her old cookery book. She had to telephone her neighbour and ask her to come and help.

Loss of linguistic ability – aphasia

Many people with dementia experience problems expressing themselves verbally. They struggle to find the right words. Some people have difficulties in understanding what others are saying, or lose their ability to read, or are unable to understand what they are reading.

Aphasia involves deterioration in using and understanding words, and includes three different types of speech problems (Engedal and Haugen 1996):

- difficulty in forming whole sentences (motor aphasia)

- difficulty in understanding what others are saying, or in understanding written text (sensory aphasia)

- naming problems (anomic aphasia).

Laura tried to explain that she had been awarded the Royal Order of Merit: 'I received that round thing which hangs from the man who was sick'. This was just after King Olav had had a stroke. She also said that she was nervous about her medical examination. She said that she feared she was unable to explain herself properly to the doctor. She struggled to find the right words.

In later stages of dementia, the spoken word can deteriorate further. There is a loss of vocabulary, and many words cannot be understood. It is often difficult to understand what the person is saying. It is important for staff to remember that the possibility of understanding the message the person is trying to convey improves when we know their background history, interests and normal reactions. Perhaps it is enough to recognize a name, or just a single word, to succeed.

The ability to understand what is being said can be impaired. We have to express ourselves clearly with few words. Instead of saying 'If you like, I could get you another cup of coffee', it might be easier for the patient to understand: 'Do you want coffee?' We can make the question easier to understand by visualizing what we are talking about, by holding up the coffee cup, or showing the coffee jug.

> Larry does not answer a question about whether he wants one type of cheese or another on his bread. When he is offered both types of cheese in front of him on the table, he has no doubt about which one he prefers.

Loss of the ability to interpret – agnosia

The ability to understand what is happening in the environment is dependent on sight, hearing and other senses giving us the correct message. *Agnosia* means a decline in the ability to recognize objects, sounds and smells despite intact senses of sight, hearing, smell and taste.

The sound of the coffee jug boiling over, the water running from a tap left on, or the smell of a burnt pan on the cooker, are generally easily identified by healthy people. When a person loses the ability to recognize such sounds and smells, it can easily lead to practical and dangerous everyday problems. Agnosia can also interfere with the ability to recognize what you see, for instance people's faces.

> Ingrid is continually occupied by the floral pattern on her skirt. She interprets the pattern as flecks, which she wants to get rid of.

> Larry rolls up the place mat, which is under his plate. He does not understand what it is for, and it is clearly a distraction to him during the meal.

Impaired ability to do practical tasks – apraxia

Apraxia means impaired ability to fulfil practical tasks despite the person being otherwise physically able, and with full understanding of what has to be done. The cause of impaired ability to manage activities of daily living, which is found in many patients with dementia, is usually more complex than apraxia. There can be loss of psychological skills needed for planning, organizing and solving practical problems. There can be loss of, for example, memory, understanding sensory experiences, and visuospatial functioning. Thus deterioration in ability to carry out activities of daily living is more understandably a result of the multi-impairment caused by a dementia illness (Andersen and Holthe 1994; Engedal and Haugen 1996).

> Astrid wants to lay the table, but does not manage to do it. She does not know where to place plates and cutlery. When she is dressing in the morning, she remains standing, confused, with her skirt around her knees, unable to progress in dressing.

It is important that staff who work in dementia care learn about the illness so that we are able to recognize the symptoms and difficulties people have in managing their practical daily tasks. Without such knowledge it is difficult to understand people's behaviour and their inability to manage the most simple things. It is easy to become irritated when a resident empties a cup of tea over the table, or takes all the slices of bread at once. Reactions to such behaviour can quickly reflect the way we respond to naughty children. Our tolerance for the patient's behaviour, which is caused by illness, increases when we learn how the illness affects skills. With this knowledge, we are in a better position to offer guidance and encouragement and to prevent unfortunate episodes.

Deterioration in attention

Attention is a basic mental ability, which deteriorates with dementia illness. Lowering of a person's level of attention will give rise to loss of the ability to manage and handle, for example in relation to problem solving and memory (Engedal and Haugen 1996). Among people with dementia, one often finds that the ability to separate important from unimportant stimuli is reduced. The filter that is normally used to focus attention on what one wants to hear or see has gone. It becomes difficult for the person to concentrate on one thing when several other activities are going on at the same time.

Peter became restless at mealtimes when he sat with other residents around the large dining table. He commented on the appearance and behaviour of both other residents and staff in a negative way and the atmosphere at the table became tense and uncomfortable. In order to protect Peter from all the impressions he received when he sat in the large group, it was decided that he should eat his meals in his room together with an assistant. This was a better solution for everyone. Peter was then able to concentrate on what he was eating. He was able to participate in social interaction, but not when he needed to use his whole attention for eating at the same time.

The staff often forget, or are not aware of how disturbing radio, television, people coming and going, noise from the kitchen machines and discussions among staff members can be. Too many distractions that cannot be sorted out lead to increased disturbance, restlessness and a general decline in completing tasks.

Different categories of attention

Focused attention is the ability to focus on one thing over time. Examples can be eating lunch without being reminded to eat, or following a television programme.

Divided attention is the ability to concentrate on several things at the same time. An example of this is the ability to eat, and also understand and participate in the conversation at the table.

Anthony becomes irritated and stops eating when Astrid, who is sitting beside him, asks if he has a new jacket on today, and where he bought it.

Neglect is another form of loss of attention. It is seen as unawareness of things on a person's right or left side.

Sylvia constantly removes the napkin of the person sitting next to her at the lunch table. She is unaware that her own napkin lies on the left-hand side of her plate. She ignores the marmalade, which is placed to the left of her at the breakfast table.

Psychological changes

Anxiety, depression, uncertainty and a tendency to be isolated

People with dementia constantly experience failure and inadequacy. They can no longer control daily tasks and challenges. Life becomes dangerous and unpredictable. Loss of skills and experiences of helplessness will easily lead to anxiety, depression and withdrawal.

> Johanna is confused and upset about the nursing home staff who will not let her go home to her husband. She has forgotten that her husband died two years ago, and she has no idea of being unable to manage at home. She often forgets where she is. She regards the people around her as strangers who prevent her from getting to her own home. Sometimes she says that she wishes she was dead.

Loss of judgement and changed behaviour

Occasionally there is a loss of the inhibition that controls behaviour and speech. Reactions and behaviour can be experienced as threatening and painful. When a person's behaviour changes, it is important to understand that this could be caused by the dementia disease. It is especially important to allow relatives the opportunity to talk about their experiences of the changed behaviour, and to help them understand that this can be part of the illness picture.

> Mary calls for her mother when she is frightened or feels abandoned. When the staff want to help her to go to the toilet, or do some other necessary task for her care, she may hit out at them.

> Jenny swears and slams doors demonstratively when she does not get the full attention of the staff. She is not bothered that other residents also need help.

> Shirley takes out her dental plate and lays it on the lunch table during the meal. Sometimes she wipes her nose with the hem of her skirt.

Most people with dementia are not in a position to evaluate their own need for help. Many will try to conceal their declining abilities. In order to avoid disclosure they refuse offers of help or are dismissive about their needs.

> Clara used to be an independent, smartly dressed and respected woman. When she was admitted to the nursing home, it was obvious that she had not been changing her clothes or washing herself for weeks. She reacted strongly against being helped with personal care during the first few days of her stay in the home. She was suspicious and acted as if she felt degraded. Her helpers had to understand that she managed this herself and she told us, if we insisted on seeing her naked, this was inevitably to embarrass her. The way she expressed this was very different from her earlier behaviour and use of language.

Delusions

Sometimes the person with dementia talks to people who are not present, or organizes imaginary objects. Such periods with hallucinations come and go. This can be the reason why the person suddenly has periods of suspiciousness, anger or restlessness.

Neurological symptoms

Neurological symptoms in dementia illnesses can include disturbances in co-ordination, balance problems and a tendency to fall. Parkinsonian symptoms, such as stiffness, tremor, slowing of tempo and deterioration in mobility, can be present to a varying degree. Some of the neurological symptoms can be side-effects of medication.

Restlessness

Restlessness and anxiety are often seen among people with dementia. Restless residents constantly wander in the corridors with no definite aim. Lack of confidence and fixed points in life makes existence insecure. 'Where am I?' 'Why am I here?' 'Who are all these strange people?' 'What will happen to me?' It is not difficult to imagine that questions like these cause feelings of restlessness. Restlessness and uneasiness can also be caused by the urge to go to the toilet, pain and discomfort, boredom or a lack of stimulation. Some dementia patients are especially vulnerable to events and can become stressed when they get tired from being exposed to too much stimulation (Øvereng 2000).

> Johanna became restless and began to shout when she took part in the Easter Sunday breakfast with other residents and staff in the department. Normally she had her meals with three other residents and a member of staff. The large table with 15 people interacting together was too much for her. She was unable to enjoy the lovely Easter buns that the staff had arranged with the residents. When all the others around the table began to sing, Johanna became agitated and unwell. She shouted and wanted to leave the table.

Restlessness is infectious. This is clearly seen when staff are busy and tend to run in the corridor. This often leads to restlessness among the residents. Mealtimes can be more peaceful if the staff sit down with the residents.

Inactivity

People with dementia illness experience problems in carrying out activities on their own (Raune 1994; Villemoes Sørensen 1997). The loss of mental capacity and deteriorating skills to plan or manage practical functions lead to reduced initiative. Very few people with dementia manage to stick to meaningful activities. They are dependent on supportive staff who can encourage and guide them, and not least participate with them. Without the initiative from others they remain sitting inactively or wander around aimlessly.

Caring needs

The caring needs of people with dementia are often great, many times greater than it may seem at first. It is easy to be misled by their appearance of being physically healthy and fit. Persons suffering from dementia are likely to have lost the ability to care for themselves, and need help and guidance in most of the activities of daily living. They can be so forgetful and disorientated that they are dependent on supervision for 24 hours a day.

> Peter was a big problem for the night staff in the nursing home. He stood up in the middle of the night and was angry and threatening when they came to help him back to bed. When Peter was admitted to the psychogeriatric department because of his difficult behaviour, it was soon obvious that he was not able to find his way to the toilet. He also had impaired skills for practical tasks, and was unable to use the toilet without anyone to guide him. The night staff in the nursing home could not understand how a man who was so physically fit and spoke so well, could have such a problem in orientating himself and in managing practical tasks. They did not see that Peter was confused when he had to get up at night and that he needed help to get to the toilet.

A care plan should be based on the degree of disability of each individual and their resources in self-care with daily activities. Good care ought to be a mixture of guidance to let the resident use his or her remaining skills, and the necessary help and support. The patients must have security, so that their daily needs for food, personal care, stimulation and rest are met. Care should be carried out in such a way that it is tailored to the individual patient's personality and preserves their dignity.

> Anna describes her need for care when she says to a member of staff that she needs help to find her way to the toilet: 'Now you must help me so that I don't disgrace myself.' There have been occasions when Anna had to sit down in the corridor because she did not get to the toilet on time. Sometimes she could not readjust her clothing after she had been to the toilet. The experience of doing something shameful is powerful and painful, even for a person who suffers from a dementia illness.

In order to provide good care it is necessary to have knowledge about the person who is ill and the ways in which the illness has affected him or her. This helps us to recognize the symptoms and loss of skills, and the way these are expressed in the resident's personality, habits and needs. Care can be helping to change a soiled blouse or to help someone through mealtimes. Help may be needed to wash hands or wipe a person's mouth after the meal. There is a 'need for care' when patients can no longer tackle their daily activities or maintain their dignity.

Treatment for people with dementia

To date there is no medication that can stop the development of a dementia illness, although there are now drugs available that can be effective in retarding the development of symptoms. Research has shown that functioning can be influenced by adaptation of the patient's environment and by an approach to care that takes account of reduced mental capacity (Haugen 1981). Several studies have shown that deteriorating skills which result from dementia can be delayed when residents are provided with suitable accommodation and care (Judd, Marshall and Phippen 1998). In Sweden it was found that 'group living' in small units for people with dementia, with permanent staff, preserved levels of functioning better than for residents who lived in large, open nursing home departments (Annerstedt 1993). The idea behind such an arrangement is to improve the residents' possibility to recognize and understand, and to reduce their experience of disturbance, insecurity and anxiety. An extension of this approach is that people with dementia function best when they have the opportunity to relate to others, and are allowed to participate at their own level (Bråne 1988; Hanserkers 1987; Haugen 1981; Lillesveen 1989; May 1998).

A literature search of environmental initiatives for older residents with dementia in institutions was carried out in 1981. The aim of the initiatives was to expose the increasing deterioration in abilities that is caused by a dementia illness. Initiatives in the following areas had an effect on residents' functioning (Haugen 1981):

- improving orientation

- increasing stimulation and activity

- increasing social interaction with other residents, relatives and staff

- making the environment as normal as possible.

This knowledge is widespread, and its principles should form the basis of the planning and treatment of people with dementia in different types of residence.

It has been shown that levels of functioning in people with dementia can be maintained by continuity in carrying out treatment plans. This means that activity programmes that have been started must continue over time (Haugen 1981; Lillesveen 1989; Riis 1986, 1987).

> In one project a group of eight residents with severe dementia and behaviour difficulties was gathered for activities with two members of staff for one hour, five days a week. The activities included singing, movement to music, making waffles and drinking coffee and just being together. Measurements of skill levels on the GBS dementia scale (Bråne 1997) were recorded at the starting point, then after four and six months, using the same group activity. The results showed that the residents' skills improved. They were less restless and confused. However, the improvement was not noticeable in the GBS index at the four month assessment. It took longer than four months before one could see a positive effect of the intervention. This shows the importance of not giving up too early, and that patients with dementia need time and continuity (Lillesveen 1989).

The main focus of treatment for people suffering from dementia should be to enable the individual to function at the highest possible level in relation to the limits imposed by their illness (Brækhus 1999). They need to practise their remaining skills. The basis of such an aim is to start planning activities that occur daily, within 'daily care plans'. It is a challenge for staff to identify the therapeutic potential in everyday activities (Archibald 1993). Food and mealtimes are well-suited activities, because everyone can relate to food and cookery.

Laying the table together

We need food every day. Mealtimes represent activities we just have to relate to

Residents can share tasks with the staff – laying the table, wiping down the sink unit, doing the dishes, peeling potatoes, kneading dough, passing the coffee jug, baking scones, placing them in the oven, and so on. Some can participate as spectators; 'It is a pleasure to have you keeping me company while I lay the table, Anna!' Others can take part as advisers: 'What do you think, Johanna, should I put more flour in the scone mixture?' 'Have we made the coffee too weak today, Anna?' Individuals must have a chance to take part in the work according to their capacity.

Mealtimes represent an essential part of the general activity in a care unit. They can provide the best means to create 'predictable activity situations' in which residents can participate every day. The way we help the residents at mealtimes is of great importance for maintaining their ability to eat. This theme will be extended later.

CHAPTER 3

Mealtimes Used as a Purposeful Activity

In a care unit mealtime activities are repeated continually during the course of the day. The day is structured by meals: breakfast, morning coffee/tea, lunch, mid-afternoon coffee/tea, supper and late evening drinks. They mark the time and divide the day into sections. This is important in the daily rhythm for older people who live in residence. Food and meals should be something to look forward to and plan for. Within this rhythmic cycle, they provide continuity and variation (Thorsen 1993).

It was mentioned earlier that functioning abilities of people with dementia are best maintained when they are actively using their remaining skills. The activities should be recognizable and repeated over time. With this background, meals offer many possibilities for purposeful activity, both as environmental therapy and as a starting point for observation of the resources and activity levels of the individual patient.

Some important aims in environmental stimulation for people with dementia can include:

- repetition and recognition

- ability to manage

- improved orientation in time, personal identity, place and situation

- stimulating the senses

- social stimulation, well-being and confidence

- observation and evaluation of function.

Repetition and recognition

Meals provide good opportunities for activities and situations that are repeated over time. When the same group of people eat together, in the same room and around the same table, this provides an essential framework for recognition. The number of people who eat together ought not to exceed what the residents can recognize from day to day; more than six or seven people can easily create confusion. Residents can have permanent places at the table. The table can be laid with a tablecloth in a distinctive colour. The cups and plates could have a distinctive pattern, and the table could be laid in a consistent manner, for example with place mats. In this way, one can build a set of routines in relation to meals that provide residents with the feeling of something they recognize and that is known to them. Recognition is a type of managing strategy that can provide a basis for security.

The practical and social environment is particularly important in enabling residents to make use of their abilities and manage generally at their own level. (Annerstedt 1993; Bull and Magnus 1996; Holthe 1998; Holthe *et al.* 1996).

The residents ought to be provided with information from their surroundings to enable them to recognize where they are and what the expected activity is. The furnishings and the atmosphere in the dining room, together with the way staff interact with the residents, are important factors in environmental therapy.

A homely atmosphere in the kitchen or dining room enables residents to feel at home rather than in a room which is furnished like a café or a canteen. Perhaps we should not to be so quick to remove everything that would normally be visible in the kitchen, but let residents see the chopping board, the coffee jug, the salt and pepper cellars, cookery

Homelike atmosphere in the kitchen

books and other things that belong in a kitchen. What we want most of all, is for residents to feel at home and feel secure. 'When the patients feel that they are secure, they can be motivated to participate actively, and take part as social individuals' (Annerstedt, in Holthe *et al.* 1996, p.33).

The way staff members participate at mealtimes is very important for the aim of making mealtimes a meaningful activity. It is the staff who have to take the initiative to create the atmosphere at the table. It is up to the staff to decide what is normal, and how the meals are to be conducted. It is important to have a common attitude concerning how much time is available, how much help each individual resident needs, how to deal with restlessness, how to set limits and when to intervene when someone makes a mess at the table. When residents are ready to eat, how many staff members eat with them? Which individuals need special support during meals and who takes responsibility for this? Who needs a member of staff to sit beside them? Such questions have to be considered in order to provide both the residents and the staff with a basis for a nice, quiet meal.

The food, as such, is also something to recognize. Many dishes that were common in households earlier have been replaced with more international food. This influences to a greater or lesser degree the menu in the nursing home. If it is possible, one can try to influence the variety of the menu. We can discuss menus with the kitchen staff and invite them to make food that used to be traditional for the residents. There is a phrase that says: 'All good food is good.' Perhaps the taste of 'shepherd's pie, like we had at home' and other dishes that are associated with good memories, is even better. The important thing is that the food stimulates the appetite, and that the resident wants to eat and feels at home while doing so.

Ability to manage

There is an emphasis on preserving remaining skills in a person with dementia. Eating is one of the skills that is preserved the longest, and it ought to be natural to consider the arrangement and content of meals as a means of enabling people with dementia to preserve their ability to eat.

To feed oneself is important for the feeling of managing one's own situation. A great deal can be done so that meals to a greater extent can provide positive experiences of individual accomplishment. First, the staff ought to be familiar with the residents' individual capacity and needs for help. This should be borne in mind when inviting residents to participate in the activities in the kitchen and dining room. This can include helping to lay the table, washing up, cleaning the table and the floor after meals, managing to butter a piece of bread, slice cheese, pass dishes, pour coffee and to use the sugar bowl. Every meal has many possibilities. It is important that the staff see these possibilities and have a common understanding about how and why they should use them.

Difficulties in managing become noticeable when one eats with others. Most people react to a lack of table manners and someone making a mess of eating at the table. The way in which people eat is noticed and perhaps remarked on. Peter, who sometimes eats out of the jam dish or drinks from the milk jug, experiences negative reactions both from other residents and from the staff: 'Twits like him should stay at home.' It is difficult to protect the residents from bullying from other residents, thus it is important to make provisions for the ones who need

A time and a chance to make use of eating abilities

assistance at the table and to have a member of staff sitting beside them to give necessary help.

> Simon sits staring at his slice of bread and is unable to organize his knife and butter and to spread anything on the bread. Finally he eats the bread dry and perhaps notices that it is not right. This is another reminder of his own incapacity. The experience and the taste could have been quite different if someone had helped him. Perhaps he only needed a question about what he wanted to put on the bread to remind him of what he should do. The way in which we help people with dementia carry out independent tasks contributes to their sense of either coping or being a failure.

The staff should arrange themselves around the table according to which residents need support. It is necessary to be flexible in evaluating what kind of help is needed. Skills maintained can vary from day to day. The staff need to focus on what the patients are doing and consistently adjust their expectations of what residents are able to do, and come to their aid when it is apparent that it is necessary. Two examples can illustrate this:

> Astrid is physically fit, but has lost the ability to organize practical tasks, and has difficulty in expressing herself. She has been a well-groomed, meticulous person of regular habits. She puts great emphasis on social companionship and likes to be involved in conversation. But when the demands around her become too great, she develops a tense facial expression, becomes restless and often wanders away from the table.
>
> If Astrid is going to manage her meals, she needs varying degrees of help. She can help herself to a piece of bread when someone offers it to her. Sometimes she can spread butter and jam on the bread herself when these are by her side. Often, she cannot find the knife to get started. Then it is important to be aware of this and offer her help. On some occasions it is sufficient for her to see how those who are sitting beside her butter their bread. At other times she has to have butter put on the knife and then can continue on her own. Sometimes Astrid needs help to butter the whole piece of bread.
>
> If someone asks Astrid what she wants on her bread, she is unable to answer. It is better to show her the items and ask her which one she wants. Sometimes the staff have to make decisions for her. We have often seen that when Astrid receives help with practical tasks that she cannot sort out herself, without being directly confronted by her own inadequacy, she is more relaxed. She participates in the social discussion at her own level of competence. It is clear that she appreciates meals in a far better way, as long as she is not confronted with practical tasks she can no longer manage.
>
> Peter is physically incapacitated in addition to suffering from advanced dementia. He cannot walk without support and sometimes uses the wheelchair at the table. In his working life, he had a responsible position and has been accustomed to being respected as the one who makes decisions. He has poor speech and is no longer able to find the words to express his wishes, or to make a coherent contribution to a conversation. He eats on his own more or less

We must give a helping hand when it seems necessary

successfully. He may spill food, put the bread in the milk glass or eat jam with his fingers.

When he has spilt food on his clothes, he often resists help in changing or tidying up. There are occasions when he becomes angry and strikes out. Peter puts great emphasis on being treated with respect. He likes to shake hands, and he smiles and nods when someone sits and talks to him. Social companionship and courtesy clearly have a positive meaning for him. At the breakfast table, Peter sometimes sits on an ordinary chair, at other times he uses a wheelchair. Some days the staff quickly spread butter and jam on two slices of bread for him and place a cup of tea at his side. On other days he is provided with the bread plate and butters bread laboriously and nicely after having had butter and jam given to him in the correct sequence. He needs plenty of time, some reminders, and attentive staff in order to manage.

There are times when he remains sitting with butter on the knife, which he finally spreads over the plate. Perhaps he dips the piece of bread in the jam dish and pushes the bread around the plate. Fellow patients react with insults. This quickly becomes a shameful situation for Peter, and causes unrest at the table.

Mealtimes provide opportunities for being together

There are a few things the staff can do to help Peter when he eats so that his experience becomes a positive one. He should sit by the table at the best possible angle, so that he makes as little mess as possible. The wheelchair should only be used in case of need, because it may strengthen the impression of Peter being helpless and make the helpers forget that he is actually able to feed himself. It doesn't take much to prevent him from trying himself. Perhaps using a napkin or an apron could help, so that he doesn't spoil his clothes. One can address him by name when offering milk and sugar or help in other ways. He needs time. It is important to come to the rescue when it is obvious that he is not managing the situation and is perhaps at risk of getting into a row with others at the table. Meals can be used to provide him with social companionship and attentiveness, which perhaps we do not manage in the course of the day.

The correct method of taking care of an individual person's needs to help them cope with meals will depend on the conditions at the time. Staff have a number of possible ways in which to positively influence the conditions.

Staff can ensure that everyone is sitting comfortably at the table, that there is good lighting, and that everyone has enough space. In our enthusiasm to help it is easy to forget that people with dementia need *time*. They need time to become orientated, to understand what has been said and to do things themselves. We can ensure that cups and glasses are not filled to the brim and in this way avoid tremulous hands spilling their contents.

We can ensure that the room is quiet. Turning off the radio and the television and closing the door will help to avoid disturbances to the residents when they are concentrating on eating.

As helpers we also ought to think about the things we can do ourselves to provide peace and quiet for people with a dementia illness. How loudly and how much do we talk? Do we talk to each other, or do we have our focus on the residents? Do we sit peacefully at the table, or do we get up and walk about?

It is important to obtain information about the resident's earlier eating habits to be aware of the food preferences and dislikes of each individual in our care.

John must have a saucer under his coffee mug, so that he can drink the warm coffee from the saucer as he has always done.

Patricia cuts her bread into small pieces at breakfast as well as slicing up fruit before eating it. For staff who are unaware of this, it is easy to mistakenly remove the knife and prevent her from eating the way she is used to.

It is important to come to the rescue of a person who is not managing a situation and is about to behave inappropriately at the table. Making minimal fuss in connection with such episodes should reduce the feelings of inadequacy among those affected. The staff can learn from 'accidents' that happen frequently. A readily available extra tablecloth and napkins can avoid the fuss when someone has spilt tea all over the table.

Sipping coffee the way you always did

Peter empties his water glass over his dinner plate. It flows over onto the table and everything looks repulsive. Karen, who is sitting on the other side of the table, observes Peter and says reproachfully: 'Look at him! He eats like a pig! I lose my appetite with people like him.' Peter stirs the messy dinner with his fork. He is unable to ask for help or sort out the mess. At this point, it is important for staff to recognize the situation, remove the plate and give him a new one, so that he can continue his meal. When staff see that Peter is unable to manage both food and drink, they ought to sit down beside him and give him necessary guidance for the rest of the mealtime.

Some people with dementia have lost their inhibitions and judgement, and may for different reasons conduct themselves inappropriately at the table. In such cases it may be best to help them to leave the table and continue the meal in their room or in other more sheltered surroundings. The staff then set the limits for the residents in order to maintain their social integrity and dignity (Rokstad *et al.* 1996)

The way in which staff deal with the situation when they have to set limits is of importance to the resident's feeling of inadequacy and shame. It is important to have in mind that one is dealing with adults who, because of chronic brain disease, are unable to evaluate either their own or other situations. Defining limits and taking action according to these limits, provides security and structure for the residents (Rokstad *et al.* 1996).

Improved orientation in time, personal identity, place and situation

Many people with dementia have problems in orientation. They may be unaware of the time of day, what day of the week it is, or the season. They don't know where they are, cannot find out how to get to the dining room without assistance. Some have difficulties in providing an account of their family, or places and events that have been important in their lives before they became ill. At times, some individuals can even become unsure of their own name. In daily contact and care of people with dementia it is necessary to find ways in which we can improve their orientation and so reduce confusion and uncertainty.

'Reality orientation' is a method of dealing with this. In practice it means 'naming the objects, actions, surroundings and current time when we interact with the elderly' (Heap 1996). Meals provide many opportunities to arrange things and approach the people with dementia in a 'reality orientating' way.

Time

Meals occur at regular intervals and convey a structure to the day. By naming the meal to which we are inviting people, they will be reminded about the time of day. There is a difference between saying, 'it is time to eat' and saying 'now it is breakfast time.' Using different types of china can differentiate weekdays and weekends. A special cloth on the table can distinguish between ordinary and special days.

When sitting round the table, we have good opportunities to talk about the day and perhaps look at the calendar. By looking out through the window at the weather and the signs of nature, the time of year can be discussed. The table can be decorated with flowers and twigs, typical for the season. Catkin, birch, white anemone, daffodils, wild flowers, rose, sweet pea, twigs with autumn leaves, rowan twigs with the red berries, Christmas flowers and so on. The selection is vast! The food itself can also hint at the season. Rhubarb, cured ham, and strawberries with cream may give associations with summer. Mutton and cabbage stew, stewed apple and jelly cream remind us of autumn, while spare ribs, sausages and pickled pork may be associated with December. In Norway, many families have traditions linked to food on festive days. Although traditions can be different from area to area, this is a subject that provides many themes for conversation. These themes then provide associations with earlier experiences and can remind people of the time of year and the current season.

Personal identity

When the same group of people meet around the same table at regular times in the course of a day, this provides a basis for recognition and group identity. It is hoped that residents gradually have the feeling of being in the right place, with the right people.

Identity is linked to a person's name. To be addressed by name strengthens consciousness of personal identity. We therefore ought to use the names of residents as often as possible. There is a difference between saying, 'Would you like more coffee?' or 'Oscar, would you like more coffee?' Table cards with easily legible names can be another way of strengthening awareness of name and identity.

Awareness of personal identity and integrity is connected with the memory of personal life history. In conversations at the meal table, we can use the present situation to encourage people with dementia to look back and remember themselves in their heyday.

> 'Sophie, this tasty cheese is good, but probably not as good as the cheese you used to make when you looked after the cows in the mountains?' This can be an introduction to remind Sophie, who had many years' experience as a milkmaid, about what we know she has been capable of. Perhaps with the help of some trigger sentences, she can tell us about cheese making and caring for animals.

'Julie, we are many around this table, but there must have been even more people for you to cater for when you had to provide for the pupils at the forestry school and see that they had good and adequate food every day.' Julie, who used to be the cook at a boarding school, has lost most of her language since she became ill. She nods and smiles and says: 'Yes, yes, yes, that's so.'

Place and situation

The behaviour of people with dementia is related to their understanding of the situation they are in. Many health workers are positively surprised the first time they go to a coffee shop with residents. This is a situation that is easily recognized, and that brings back previously learnt social skills. Persons with dementia do what they have been accustomed to do when they were in town having a coffee. This will also occur in the nursing home. By preparing meals similar to the ones people have been accustomed to at home, they find it easier to recognize and understand the situation and conduct themselves correctly (Dent 2000).

Johanna and Larry are having dinner at a little table in the corridor of the nursing home, while staff rush about. Most of them say 'Hello' or 'Does it taste good?' as they pass. Very soon, Johanna gets up and says that she has to catch the bus home. She leaves her half-eaten dinner plate. Larry looks at the food on his plate and at Johanna who walks away. He does not know what he ought to do.

A table that is laid in a dining room where people sit and eat together, provides a far better fixed point for understanding the situation in the current time and place.

A table laid for breakfast offers many challenges for focusing on orientation skills. How does the butter and other items on the table look, and what should be used first and last? To stimulate orientation one can ask residents to pass things on the table: the butter, the milk, the bread. This will make them aware of the items around them.

The staff often forget that older people generally need more time than others to become orientated in order to perform expected actions.

We are as a rule too quick to interfere and help before they have had the chance to organize themselves.

> Shirley asks Johanna to pass the sugar at the breakfast table. Johanna concentrates, puts down her slice of bread and looks for the sugar bowl. Before she has a chance to reach out for the sugar, a helpful member of staff who is sitting between the two women passes the sugar bowl to Shirley. Johanna looks round her as though she does not quite understand the situation.

Stimulating the senses

Food appeals to many senses. It can be attractive to look at, we can smell it, and it has a taste. It can awaken associations and sensations. The sight and smell of food help people to decide if they are full or hungry. These associations can awaken the expectation and urge for something good, and can provide the feeling of having had something that was enjoyable.

The way food is served, how it smells, and its appearance, will influence the feelings and associations that are being stimulated. These associations are as important for people with dementia as they are for healthy people.

The smell of newly made coffee, freshly baked bread, biscuits or cakes, fried bacon and eggs, and simmering lamb stew stimulates associations with the past and expectations of an enjoyable experience.

A plate of carefully arranged sandwiches will be appreciated, and many will help themselves to an extra piece. The sight of an attractively laid table with flowers and a decorated cake creates an atmosphere and raises expectations. It can strengthen anticipation, and make people aware that something is going to be celebrated .

Food offers great possibilities for stimulating recognition, using the senses of smell and taste. 'Was the coffee too strong?' 'Too hot?' 'What type of fruit is this jam made from, could it be blackcurrant?'

In units where the kitchen and equipment for preparing food are on site, there are possibilities of providing sensual experiences with food similar to the ones people were accustomed to at home. People with dementia can then participate in preparing the food: chopping vegetables, scrubbing potatoes or stirring the sauce. The smell of dinner will spread around the rooms and stimulate appetite. They can hear that the potatoes are boiling and recognize the smell of meat cooking. The senses can be used in normal, well-known situations and surroundings.

Social stimulation, well-being and confidence

Food is traditionally something to gather for, something we look forward to. The social companionship around the table, and the possibility of using it for conversation and contact between people, is in itself a positive element that can stimulate both well-being and appetite. In many cases, it is not what we eat, but who we eat with, that decides our level of well-being and perhaps also how much we eat (Archibald *et al.* 1994; Malone 1996).

Social passivity is a typical feature of behaviour in people with dementia. The person with a dementia illness speaks less, has little initiative and is less involved than before he or she became ill. Investigations have shown that the surroundings and the way the room is organized during meals are vital for the social interactions between residents and staff, and between the residents themselves (Melin and Götestam 1981; Davies and Snaith 1980). All indications showed that people with dementia who sit together round a smaller table at meals, relate to each other and to staff to a much greater extent than those who sit in rows or along the wall in the sitting room, with food served to them on a tray.

Every time staff sit down and eat together with the residents, they provide an opportunity to stimulate conversation and contact at the table. For people with dementia it is easiest to talk about things that can be seen and experienced in the present. It is more difficult to recall things that happened the day before. It is, in other words, better to talk about what is being eaten today than to discuss yesterday's dessert.

The food and whatever occurs at mealtimes, offer many topics for conversation. It can include everything on the table, whether the bread is sliced too thickly, which type of sugar one prefers to use, or what type of meat we are having for supper today. Has anyone at the table ever been a farmer? Perhaps a farming story will be recalled.

Patients need encouragement and initiative from the staff to participate in the conversation

We should talk together in such a way that the persons with dementia feel that they are included in the group. In the book *Live the Forgetful Life* the author says: 'We need to experience that others see us, and to be appreciated as unique individuals and not just one in the crowd. This need does not cease when a person gets a dementia illness' (Aremyr 1993, p.34).

Staff conversation can often be of a private nature, but it is acceptable if we share what we experienced out in town the previous evening in a way that means everyone sitting at the table can be part of the story. A little gossip and a suggestive story can be engaging and spice up the day for most people.

Residents have lost their daily means of associating with friends and family. This causes feelings of loss, bereavement and uncertainty. The staff have an important role in acting as substitutes for those who earlier in life were daily contacts and supporters. The residents still need someone to talk to, to trust and confide in, someone to complain to, and someone to make them laugh. This is important for the feeling of well-being and security (Wogn-Henriksen 1997).

Having a good laugh with somebody

Weekdays in the nursing home are often divided up and busy. Thus it is important to use the meal times to sit down and be together and associate with each other.

Observation and assessment of functioning skills

In order to plan the treatment and care of people with dementia, it is necessary to identify the type of dementia and the degree of cognitive impairment. This is done through different types of medical and psychological investigations (Engedal and Haugen 1996). Mapping how the patient manages general practical daily tasks is another necessary and important part of dementia assessment. This assessment is mainly done by the staff in the home where the resident is living.

To participate in a meal demands the use of many different skills. Here the staff have natural periods of daily observations of the residents' functional abilities in well-known activities. This can provide a useful basis for cross-disciplinary discussion about resources, functioning ability and the need for care. It will also provide a necessary supplement to other investigations that have been done in order to establish

Mealtimes are occasions for observing resources and deficiencies

the diagnosis and plan further management. The observations, which are made by the staff, can be systematically recorded in a specifically designed 'OBS-dementia form' (Haugen *et al*. 1997). The form should to be completed by staff who know the person, after they have discussed among themselves how they experience the individual's remaining skills.

> Clare lived in a special unit for people with dementia in a nursing home. The facilities and atmosphere were characterized by social interaction, pleasant mealtimes and companionship for the seven residents. Clare stood out among the residents. With her disturbed and provocative behaviour she was regarded as a problem for both staff and fellow residents. She loudly repeated what the others said, used bad language and often reacted by shouting at people who did not respond immediately. When the staff completed her OBS-dementia form, there was agreement that she was completely dependent on others for help in personal care and that she needed considerable help at meals. Her sadness and depression were recognized. She often seemed to be angry and irascible, and was continually anxious in daily

situations. She was frequently restless, and did not participate well in social interactions. It became clear to the staff that Clare had few remaining skills, and that the social interactions in the residential home were perhaps too demanding for her. When focusing on her sadness and anxiety, the staff wondered if the disturbed behaviour could be an expression of her anxiety and depression. It was decided that Clare should be protected from the distractions of the communal area and that she would spend more time in her room together with a member of staff. In this way, it could be judged if personal contact and a more sheltered environment would make her feel more secure and content.

By completing the OBS-dementia form regularly, it is possible to measure the change in level of functioning over a period of time. Changes in ability are affected by the progress of the disease, environmental factors and medication. In any case, it is important to make a good survey of functional skills and suggest expectations of what the person will be able to manage.

The following are some basic points for observation of functional skills:

- inability to complete practical tasks

- memory

- initiative

- orientation

- concentration and attentiveness

- social skills and behaviour.

Inability to complete practical tasks

As mentioned earlier, a reduced ability to carry out practical tasks is common among many residents with dementia (Andersen and Holthe, 1994). In the early stage of the illness, this may be seen as difficulty in using electrical equipment, for example the washing machine or the cooker. These are tasks that demand a variety of skills in order to achieve results. Later, as the disease progresses, the person with dementia may become unable to do less complex tasks, such as independently buttering a piece of toast, or pouring a glass of milk.

> Esther was asked to help laying the table for supper. She put all the plates on one side of the table, and looked a bit uncertainly at Joan who had asked her to help. Joan placed the plates in their right position around the table and asked Esther to put one glass with each plate. Esther still had difficulties, and put the glasses in a group on one side of the table.

Such an observation provides useful information about Esther's problems in handling practical tasks.

> When Esther eats her supper, she uses a knife and fork in the way she has always done. Now and again she looks uncertainly at the person next to her and benefits from seeing what the others do.

It is important to see that Esther is able to eat her supper with a knife and fork despite needing help and guidance at breakfast in managing her bread and butter.

> Patricia, who is a widow, was admitted to the psychogeriatric ward because of a critical situation following acute confusion at home. She had begun to throw her 'meals on wheels' in the rubbish bin, and her neighbours found her in her nightgown walking about at all hours of the day and night. In the ward it was clear that Patricia had no particular difficulties with meals. She coped so well practically and socially that the staff wondered how the problems could have become so great at home. Patricia's room was quite disorganized. She could not find her clothes when she had to get dressed in the morning. Her hairbrush and toiletries were not to be found in the bathroom, and she had no idea where to look for them. She had several bags, which she emptied and refilled, without completing what she originally was aiming to do. It was obvious that if she were left to organize herself on her own, there would be chaos.

Patricia had a structured situation at mealtimes. The table was laid; the staff welcomed people in and arranged the proceedings. Patricia ate completely independently, helped other residents and engaged herself in chat with the others around the table. She seemed secure and sociable. She needed a framework and other people who could understand and relate to her problems caused by her dementia illness.

Sometimes we see that residents cannot use cutlery and other objects on the table correctly. One person may chew his napkin, spread butter on his plate, or perhaps eat his neighbour's food. In such situations, it may be necessary to move things away from the person's area, as too many things around a person can increase confusion.

> Larry fiddled about with the cutlery, cup and glass at the breakfast table. He regularly ate with his knife, and used it in the jam jar afterwards. He would drink from his neighbour's cup and glass. When he was asked to help himself from the serving-dish, he kept the spoon. There was much confusion at the table caused by Larry's problems.

The situation improved when Larry was seated at the end of the table, a little separated from the other residents. He received milk first and then coffee later. Butter and marmalade were passed to him one at a time and removed to the centre of the table, so that he did not have so many things immediately in front of him. There was less confusion when the number of objects was reduced, and he received help in using items in the correct sequence.

Memory

The person with dementia often experiences a deteriorating memory. Although Mary was given a cup of coffee 30 minutes before breakfast, she said that she had not tasted coffee for many days.

> Louise helped to make pancakes for supper. She had no difficulty in mixing the batter if the ingredients were measured and laid out. She cooked the pancakes to a good consistency. She used the frying pan and buttered the pancakes properly. When we sat around the table,

Louise told us she really enjoyed the tasty pancakes and asked who had made them.

The conversations we have while sitting around the table give us an impression of memory problems. We can talk about the things we have experienced together, what we saw on television the previous day, whom we met when we were out walking, and what the weather was like.

For many it is easier to remember events from earlier in life – the name of the teacher at school, where fruit was collected in autumn, what it was like to run a family, build a house and participate in professional life. When we hear that people have reminiscences from their earlier life, this provides an opportunity to use memory to strengthen self-image and a feeling of identity (Heap 1996; Murphy 1994). The background information we collect from residents and from their carers should be written down, so that everyone who works in the unit has the possibility of chatting with residents about themes that are meaningful for the individual. In this way, we may help the residents to recollect experiences from the past and facilitate their long-term memory.

Orientation

Awareness that the meal is either lunch or supper is in itself a sign that a person is orientated in time of the day. Many people with dementia have lost their sense of time and have no idea what time of day it is. Many also have difficulties in knowing what day, month or season it is. In conversations at different meals, a useful subject is to talk about what time and what day it is.

Everyone is gathered for breakfast at the day centre. Before the guests and staff leave the table Johanna is asked to read what is on the information board for today. The day of the week, the date and programme for the day with times of meals and activities are read out loud. Johanna concludes by looking out of the window and commenting on the fine autumn weather. 'It is such lovely weather today, it really makes me feel good!'

Some residents have problems in orientating themselves in the unit. Some people never find the way to their own room, the sitting room or the toilet, on their own. A sign-board can sometimes be useful (Bull and Magnus 1996; Holthe 1998), but most residents who are less able to find the room and directions will need an escort.

The design and equipment in a room can support the feeling of being in the right place, for example a kitchen with cooking utensils.

In conversation at the meal table, we can chat about where we are and who we are. In this way, we can form an impression of how aware people with dementia are of their own family, where they live and their current location in the nursing home or day centre.

> Laura is 84 years old and has lived in the nursing home for two years. She walks restlessly about the corridor when Mary invites her to come for breakfast. Laura thanks Mary politely for the invitation, but says that she doesn't have the time to eat now. She says she only came in to see her sister, and that she is busy because she is going to see her mother who is ill at home and is waiting for her. She lets herself be persuaded to remain in order to have a little coffee. When she comes into the dining room and sees her fellow residents, she is amazed to meet people she knows and joins them at the table.

There was no doubt that Laura did not understand where she was or what time it was. She was occupied with her own thoughts and worries and became restless. By inviting her to breakfast, Mary could help her to change focus and become aware of something specific that was happening there and then.

Initiative

Persons with dementia are likely to become less active than before they were ill. It is rare to hear residents say they want to make biscuits, or suggest that today it is their turn to lay the supper table. Many will remain sitting a bit puzzled at the breakfast table without asking for things to be passed to them, or expressing that they cannot see their favourite sandwich spread.

Lorna is new in the home. She carefully helps herself to a piece of bread from the basket that is passed around. She does not say anything. She eats the bread without butter and jam. Mary, who is sitting beside her, asks if she would like another piece of bread and offers her the basket. She places the butter dish beside Lorna and asks her what she would like to put on her bread. Lorna says she doesn't know. Mary shows her the variety of spreads. Lorna selects jam and spreads her bread with butter and jam.

There is no doubt that Lorna needed help to cope. She had no problems in managing practical tasks, but she did not have the initiative to start or to ask for help. It was easy to understand that Lorna would receive little stimulation and have limited experience unless others helped her to manage simple tasks. Gradually as she became involved in washing up with the staff and helped to lay and clear the table, she learnt that she could continue to succeed in things and received positive attention from the others.

Concentration and attentiveness

Some residents become restless and leave the table before they have finished eating. Others fidget, spill the food and behave inappropriately.

As mentioned earlier, the ability to distinguish essential from inessential impressions is reduced with the development of dementia. Thus it is very important to evaluate if the causes of the chaotic situations we sometimes experience at mealtimes are due to the environment and setting of the meal.

Do the residents have the peace and quiet they need to compose themselves in order to eat? Do noise and other impressions distract their attention from what the staff expect them to do? When radio and television are in the vicinity of the meal table, it can become difficult to separate their sounds and pictures from what is happening around the table. People come and go. Doors are opened and closed. The restless residents do not receive the help they need. The staff talk to each other across the room and leave the table to fetch something that is missing. One can think of numerous examples of disturbance to the patients' environment that can influence their ability to concentrate. The staff are often, without being aware of it, the main source of noise during the meal.

Social skills and changed behaviour

When we sit together at meals, we can observe how people interact with each other. Some are happy with social interaction, while others cannot cope with company.

> Laura often paces up and down the corridor, searching for somebody who will help her find the exit door or order a taxi, so that she can go home. This happens regularly when she is left on her own in the unit. She has to be persuaded to come into the dining room in order to eat. When Laura has sat down at the table, she changes from being restless and irritated to becoming polite, attentive and sociable. She makes positive remarks about the food, and she chats with staff and other residents. She helps the others and comments when she sees that someone has an empty tea cup. It is obvious that she enjoys company.

> Larry sits in a wheelchair after having fractured his hip. He says that he feels bad because he can no longer move about freely. He becomes confused and angry and may strike and scold the staff who want to help him. He is a person the staff are reluctant to help. During meals, he needs someone beside him to keep things in order, give him a slice of bread and guide him in organizing his meal. The way we communicate and socialize with Larry is important to get him in the mood to collaborate. Chatting with him about former interests helps him to feel secure and calm. He then gives an impression that he feels we are in the same team, doing something together.

Both of these residents had social skills that were not easily recognized throughout the day, but could be seen when we sat together at mealtimes. This experience provides us with ideas about how we can act in the social arena to moderate undesirable behaviour.

> Peter manages to eat on his own, but it takes a long time. He has tremulous hands, and his movements are slow. His speech has

deteriorated. He is no longer able to talk in sentences. Because of his tremor and slowness, the staff offer him continuous help, but he feels they are interfering. At breakfast, it looks as though he enjoys being at the table. He responds when we say 'good morning', and he says 'thank you' when we serve him the food. He is calm and alert at this time. Lunch can be more problematic. Peter is never able to finish his meal, and he becomes angry and tired when he needs to be helped to take his midday nap. It was decided that Peter should have his lunch in his room. This took him away from all the distracting activity in the dining room, and he could be helped to take a nap in his bed immediately after his meal.

In contrast to Laura and Larry, Peter did not benefit from social companionship at the meal table. He was better off with his lunch when he was alone.

Food, mealtimes and having a meal in institutional care

> The joy of mealtimes belongs to all ages, rich and poor in all countries and at all times. The happiness at the table can be combined with other joys and remains to the end a comfort for the regrets about what we have lost. (Brillat Savarin, in Elwing 1989, p.329)

This quotation from a famous French gourmet explains how essential and meaningful food and mealtimes are for people in general. It also says that food is particularly important as a comfort for people who are elderly and ill, and who no longer have so many opportunities for pleasure in life.

Meals are used as a setting to mark big and small events in life. We gather round the dinner and coffee table with expectations and traditions (Burton-Jones 1998). When we are alone, we may go to the food cupboard and take a snack to cheer ourselves up. If someone comes to visit, the tradition in Norway is to offer the guests something to eat. Most elderly people here have been used to having a rich supply of biscuits and bread in readiness should anyone pay a visit.

When living in a nursing home, the residents with dementia often lose the initiative and ability to go and find a snack when they want to, or suggest that the family is welcome to come and have cream cakes on one's 80th birthday. Others, relatives and staff, have to look after this part of the residents' life. The way we do this means a lot for the residents' pleasure and happiness in their days in the nursing home. In Karen Blixen's short story, Babette's Feast (Blixen 1975), we are reminded that good food and drink can provide an almost magical experience. We read about a meal where the atmosphere in the room and the attitude of the guests changed from suspicion to reconciliation and harmony.

Mealtimes constitute an important part of the programme of the day in nursing homes, other forms of residential care for older people, and day centres. Mealtimes organize the day and ought to be something to look forward to. Often in our daily practice, our experience is that what could be a comfortable hour is characterized by stress and restlessness. The staff run hither and thither, and the residents do not receive the consideration they need in order to experience their meal in a positive way. It can seem in the nursing home that the first priority is to regard food as nutrition and a source of energy. Little consideration is given to the psychological, social and cultural factors that are associated with food, and how these factors influence our appetite and desire to eat (Axelsson, Nordberg and Asplund 1984).

Helping residents during meals can be regarded as a practical task like many of the other daily routines in the home or centre. Mealtimes are often characterized by effectiveness and routines. The staff become more focused on having the table cleared than on allowing the individual the possibility of enjoying the meal in peace and quiet. In an investigation into a nursing home for people with dementia in Leeds, it was found that less time was used for meals when there were more nurses on duty. They speeded up the mealtimes (Littlewood and Saeidi 1994).

The residents lose their influence over what they want to eat, how much, for how long, with whom and in which surroundings. The possibility of choice is often not there, and the residents will become more passive. The staff are at risk of distancing themselves and developing attitudes that block the possibilities to understand and meet the residents (Kittwood 1999).

A Swedish study showed that staff easily overlooked the need for autonomy in people with a dementia illness, such as making decisions for themselves (Ekman and Norberg 1988). An example from the study was that some staff assumed that all older people like the same type of music. It is not difficult to think that similar generalizations occur around old people and food.

It is not unusual to hear staff in the nursing home say with great conviction that 'the elderly like jam best', 'the elderly think that tomatoes and greens are too luxurious for everyday sandwiches', or 'the elderly would rather sit in their room and eat'. It is frightening to think how such generalizations can influence attitudes in daily life and lead us to overlook an individual's wishes and needs.

Medication in food

Medication is often given around mealtimes. Drugs may be mixed with food. An investigation into civil rights and the use of restraints in the care of people with dementia, showed that drugs were mixed with food daily or occasionally in 61 per cent of dementia care units and in 49 per cent of the ordinary units in Norwegian nursing homes (Stortingsmelding (White Paper) No. 28, 1999–2000; Engedal et al. 2000). Drugs can be put into a glass of milk, or crushed under jam on a slice of bread or mixed with jam and served on a spoon. If there are special reasons for giving drugs in this way, it is important to make the resident aware that the drug is mixed in the food. There are formal guidelines for administering drugs to people who are unable to take care of their own medication. In services for people with dementia, it is especially important to be aware of the person's right to refuse to take medication. It is illegal to give someone a drug against his or her wishes. When a drug is necessary for life, such as insulin or heart medication, the drugs can legally be given against the person's wish as a form of necessity (Nygård et al. 1994).

A temporary member of staff put gastric drugs into the milk glasses of all the residents. She had seen this drug administration being done for one resident and thought it was a good way to ensure that everyone received their medication from beakers that were often left untouched after the residents had finished their meal.

When drugs are mixed in food, this alters its taste. Perhaps the milk doesn't taste like milk any more. The slice of bread and jam does not taste as expected, but has an added flavour. In the daily activity of busy care units, it is easy to overlook such considerations. Sometimes routine approaches are used when in fact there should be individual solutions for each person. We do what we see other staff do, and think this is the way it should be done.

CHAPTER 4

The Relationship between Ideals and Practical Reality

There are many factors that influence how the serving of meals is carried out in a nursing home. Approaches to daily work in the home can be seen as a result of how the following matters are solved:

- building design

- inter-disciplinary collaboration

- prioritizing tasks

- organizing staff and residents

- staff participation and conduct at mealtimes

- knowledge, attitude and motivation.

Building design

The way in which the building has been designed influences the attitude of those who live and work there. Many nursing homes are built and equipped more like a hospital than a home. It is often evident that more consideration has been given to the efficiency of employees than to the comfort of the people living there and whose home it is. There may be

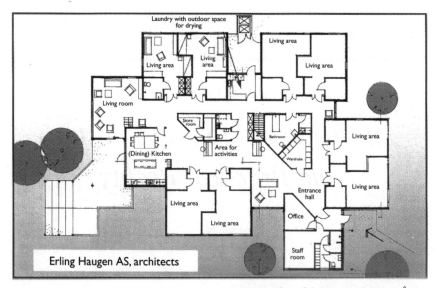

Plan of the nursing home in Årdal

long corridors and open sitting rooms with institutional furniture. The kitchen is often designed for the staff, without space for activities together with the residents.

The food is prepared in large, communal kitchens. The residents rarely have the opportunity to participate in food preparation, and to recognize the smell of food that is being prepared.

A number of recently built nursing homes have cafeterias for the residents. There they gather and eat together with many others. For people with dementia this can be a source of confusion. One is exposed to many impressions and there is hardly a homely atmosphere.

Some nursing homes are built with corridors leading to a large common room with many tables where everyone eats. One easily gets the feeling of being in a shopping centre and not in a home where people live and spend their time. In recent years there have been several reports with recommendations on planning nursing homes based on more modern principles for caring for people with dementia (Bull and Magnus 1996; Cohen and Weismann 1991; Den Norske Stats Husbank 1998; Holthe *et al.* 1996; Judd *et al.* 1998).

Furniture sets the character of a room. In many nursing homes the furniture looks more like something we expect to find in a waiting room or a public place rather than in a home. Sometimes a resident declares that he is in a big ship. One colleague said she had the feeling of being in an airport, with all the high-backed chairs of the same colour standing side by side. The art selected to decorate the walls in nursing homes often emphasizes an atmosphere that is more typical of a public area.

The fact that a nursing home environment has few homely characteristics and is more adapted to provide efficiency for staff management rather than functioning as a home for people, does something to the people who work and live there. This can mean that residents have limited opportunities for their own activities, and they become passive. The staff become efficient and willing to help. It is easy to be efficient in the helping role by doing things for everyone without taking into consideration what the individual can do on his or her own. We take the cup out of a resident's hand and give him his tea because it is quicker. We prefer to put milk in all the tea cups without thinking that some residents could manage without help and would also enjoy the satisfaction of doing it themselves.

The way in which traditional nursing homes are built often limits the possibilities for creating a homely atmosphere at mealtimes. It is easy to become frustrated about how inappropriate the facilities are, and not consider how to make the best of the situation. It is important that we do not forget the residents' situation in our dissatisfaction with rooms and furniture. We have a great challenge to find alternatives for room use to the residents' best advantage.

We don't have to let the 25 residents in the unit eat in the large dining room because the architect planned it that way. We must be creative and focus on what is best for the residents. It then becomes easier to move furniture and lamps and evaluate how the rooms can be used for other purposes than originally planned. In an interesting project in Brumunddal, the sitting room, the dining room and the activity room were rearranged into all-purpose rooms where each of the three residential groups were occupied during the day. This made it possible to offer more stable companionship for residents and staff

Mixing the ingredients for waffles at the dining table

(Lillesveen 1989). It is possible to use the dining table for making cakes and peeling potatoes if there are no better facilities.

Inter-disciplinary collaboration

Among health care staff involved in care of the elderly, there is a traditional concept that nursing staff are responsible for care and nursing, while occupational therapists, physiotherapists and activity organizers are concerned with training and promoting activity. In the care of people with dementia it is necessary to break down these distinctions and work together to achieve what is best for a normal life for the residents. Inter-disciplinary work is very important. The professions need each other's knowledge and different starting points. By taking part in meals we can all have experiences and make observations together with the residents. This gives a basis for multi-disciplinary discussions and planning of the treatment and care.

If mealtimes are to have an important place in treatment and well-being, all professions working with residents should be involved. We have to work together, agree on methods and aims and give each other reciprocal guidance and support in practical work. This can lead to changing both routines and traditional ideas about staff roles. Change is a difficult process and takes time.

When planning for people with dementia, it is especially important to organize staff in a way that takes into consideration the continuity of mealtimes. Everyone who works in the unit must be informed about the daily routines related to meals and be aware of the aims and purpose of those routines. Everyone can then take responsibility and have confidence in their work. This will change the attitude that organizing meals depends on one profession, or chosen members of staff. This is especially important in the evenings, and at weekends and holidays.

> In a unit with unstable staffing, the routine for breakfast changed from day to day. One day the table was laid for the residents and the staff, on other days it was laid just for the residents, and the staff helped themselves to a cup of tea. Some days the table was laid with bread, butter and spreads, and other days the bread was already spread with butter and jam. Some laid the table with place mats while others felt that it could confuse the residents and did not use them. There was a lot of uncertainty among the staff about organizing breakfast. Mealtimes were characterized more by accidental circumstances than being a safe and secure element of daily life in the unit. There was a lack of routines and continuity both for staff and for residents.

In order to be flexible with meals, it is necessary to work closely with staff in the main kitchen. We have to make clear to them that older people need time; and that people with dementia need even more time. It is important that they understand why staff should have and be able to allow plenty of time for meals. If there is pressure to finish eating so that the main kitchen can start the washing up, this will make us rush and deny us the valuable mealtime experience. We need time.

> The main kitchen staff had a greater acceptance of the regular requests for special services after they were invited to share a meal with the residents and staff in the dementia unit. They began to

understand what is essential to enable the residents to enjoy their meal.

It is important that the staff who are linked to the unit intermittently, for example cleaning staff, porters, janitors, doctors and chiropodists, all respect mealtimes. If the supervising doctor comes when breakfast is being served, both residents and staff will be occupied with this. A natural thing to do could be to join in with a cup of coffee and use the opportunity to observe the residents in an everyday situation.

Generally there ought to be a common goal of serving meals in an undisturbed atmosphere. An interruption in the 'middle of a meal' can lead to increased confusion and spoil the basis of a good day.

Prioritizing tasks

There are many tasks in a nursing home that have to be taken care of. If a decision is made to dedicate more time and more staff to focusing on meals, this will have consequences for other tasks. When some activities are given a higher priority, others have to take a lower priority. It is possible that there will be less time for traditional activities and routine tasks, such as keeping the unit clean and tidy.

Tasks that are measurable and visible are often regarded as the most important: 'How many did I help having a shower today?' 'How many beds have we changed today?' We talk less about how long we sat at the breakfast table, or how many people we saw who felt comfortable at the coffee time after lunch.

Perhaps we need to re-evaluate and expand our understanding of which tasks should be prioritized. What do we miss when we spend an hour having breakfast with the residents? Is anyone being neglected? What is more important? We should often discuss these sorts of questions with our colleagues.

We should speak out more openly about what we do, and what relevance we think it has for residents and colleagues. Often instead of asking, we just worry: 'I wonder what the others think of me when I sit down and have coffee with the residents instead of tidying up the linen cupboard.'

Organizing staff and residents

Organizing staff and residents is important in the care situation. Many investigations have shown that people with dementia function best in small groups with permanent staff (Annerstedt 1993, 1997; Ramsby 1985). There ought not to be more than six to eight residents in each group. Staff duty periods and work rotas should be organized so that residents have the least possible number of staff to relate to.

There may be advantages in placing residents together who are more or less on the same functional level. In the Brumunddal Project, it was found that residents improved their function and the staff became more interested and involved in their job when they were organized in this way (Lillesveen 1989).

The classification of functioning levels at meals was described by Lillesveen, Berg and Skjerven (1999, pp. 102–3) and they reported that:

> The 18 residents in the unit were divided into three groups of six, similarly impaired and in comparable need of help in daily activities. In one group, the breakfast table was laid with spreads and sliced bread. Lunch was served on a dish which was passed round. The residents managed to help themselves with the food and were helped when necessary by the staff.
>
> In the second group, the breakfast table was laid without bread and spreads but with sandwiches made in advance. Those residents who could butter their own bread, sat at an end of the table where the spreads and sliced bread were placed. In this way, they could use their remaining skills. Lunch was served plated to everyone. Some people needed help in eating and drinking. Others needed an assistant to provide practical help and care during the meal, and to maintain the focus on eating.
>
> In the third group, the large oval dining table was not laid before residents had been helped to sit around it. The meals were served with readily prepared plated food for breakfast, dinner and supper. Many needed help in eating and drinking and were dependent on having an assistant beside them, to prevent them from knocking over a cup or generally make a mess with the food.

When residents are put together with others with similar remaining skills, they can be offered the same level of activity and support. It becomes easier for the staff to enable people to participate at their own level during the meal.

A Swedish investigation of meals for people with dementia describes how the staff had greater understanding of the residents' problems when they concentrated on fewer residents (Athlin and Norberg 1987). It is not difficult to imagine that it is easier to help fewer persons than many, and that the chance of getting to know each of the residents is better. We become more involved with individuals and are in a better position to use ourselves as fellow humans in their care (Kittwood and Bredin 1992).

Staff participation and conduct at mealtimes

In Sweden, investigations have illustrated how people with dementia function at meals with staff participation (Sandman and Norberg 1988). They showed that the staff had the effect of making the residents more passive, and they did not take the residents' varying levels of disability into consideration.

Health care staff have been trained to help. In addition, they have learnt much about hygiene and the effective use of time. To sit quietly at the breakfast table and to pay attention to residents struggling with buttering their bread is not what we have learned to consider as help and effective work! A study in a dementia unit in Leeds showed that the more staff who took part in meals, the faster the meal was completed. Those who carried out the study raised the question of whether nurses regarded mealtimes mostly as a practical task and where their role was in helping the residents to finish the meal. It became clear that they did not encourage the residents to do as much as possible for themselves and to enjoy social interaction (Littlewood and Saeidi 1994).

To allow time for residents to help themselves, we have to accept minor accidents of spilling food or soiling a blouse. This is contrary to our established ideals. We remove the spoon from the hands of a resident because we think he will spill his food. We stand over someone when we help them to eat, instead of sitting down beside them. In many ways, we

There must be enough room for all

make them passive with our haste. We often find that staff cause most of the restlessness at the table; for instance by walking round the table with the basket of bread rather than sitting down and asking the residents to pass it to each other. The facilities of meals must be organized to suit both residents and staff. Is the table large enough? Is there a chair for everyone? Have we enough cutlery? The staff are poor models when they sit on an armrest and eat buttered toast from the kitchen because there is not enough crockery and cutlery or space around the table.

When staff eat with the residents, this increases the feeling of equality and experience of social interaction. The residents then have role models that can help and support them in managing their own skills at the table.

Confidence and well-being can be developed if the residents experience pleasant mealtimes. This will improve appetite and food intake.

Knowledge, attitude and motivation

We need knowledge in order to plan, carry out and evaluate the giving of proper care to people with dementia. Further education and courses can show us how to learn from our own practice. If new knowledge is going to be applied and used in daily work with residents, it is important that those who lead the unit are committed and promote development of new methods and attitudes. Staff do need to be positively motivated (Munch 1993; Rokstad *et al.* 1996).

Many studies of staff groups who work with people with dementia have shown that the efficiency of courses and training is dependent on how the staff are followed up with peer group discussions and guidance in their own working environment (Lintern, Woods and Phair 2000; Noland and Keady 1996). Professional support and guidance which have their starting point in practice are important for the experience of doing a good job. They strengthen motivation and increase commitment.

The patients with dementia are special because they are rarely able to express their own wishes and needs. And they cannot give feedback to those who help them, or report their own experiences of treatment and care. Because of the patients' declining ability to plan, remember and take care of themselves, the staff often have to make decisions on behalf of residents. We have to take on tremendous responsibility as helpers of chronically ill people. It is important that we take the opportunity to discuss and share ethical dilemmas and experiences of daily contact with residents with our colleagues and senior staff. In this way, we can help each other to put our experiences into a professional context and learn from each other. We could also help each other to be more clear about attitudes and how we relate to the residents. The attitude we have towards residents as people and fellow human beings is of vital importance for the way in which we provide care (Kittwood 1999).

It can be difficult to see results of the contribution we make from day to day. Meals can vary from the purely ideal to complete chaos. It is important to be able to understand and accept deviant behaviour as part of the illness picture. At the same time, we need knowledge and the ability to consider our own contribution to the situation. What caused something to go wrong? Did we expect too much from the resident? How did I approach the resident? How could I have done things differently?

The most important resource in the care for people with dementia is the personnel who work with them. To work with people with such an illness is psychologically demanding. We can often feel that we have exhausted our last reserves of patience, and that nothing helps. Then it is important to have the confidence and support from colleagues and to seek help to set the problems in perspective. Time to talk together, to share experiences, and to look after each other, is an important part of the job. Those who lead and organize the caring services for residents with dementia have important challenges here.

Conclusion

The care of people with dementia has different priorities in the municipality. The framework in which services are provided varies. The system of health care needs time to recognize the challenges of care for people with dementia and to accept the consequences. Those of us who work with people with dementia and who know what it demands to create a good service for this group of patients, ought to inform the administration and appropriate authorities about their needs. We also need to develop skills and competence and share experiences in order to find useful methods of working.

As stated in the introduction, the purpose of this book is to provide ideas about how meals can be used in a more purposeful way in caring for and treating people with dementia in the nursing home, sheltered housing or day centre. The principles of treatment that are described in connection with meals can also be used as a general starting point for the care and treatment of people with a dementia illness. The ultimate aim is to maximize the patients' quality of life and at the same time increase the carers' job satisfaction in the day-to-day management of this extremely challenging group of illnesses.

References

Andersen, A. and Holthe, T. (1994) *Aldersdemens – Fra sansing til handling.* Sem: INFO-banken.

Annerstedt, L. (1993) 'Development and Consequences of Group Living in Sweden'. *Social Science and Medicine 37,* 12, 1529–1538.

Archibald, C. (1993) *Activities 2.* Scotland: Dementia Development Services Centre, University of Stirling.

Archibald, C., Carver, A., Kene, J. and Watson, R. (1994) *Food and Nutrition in the Care of People with Dementia.* Scotland: Dementia Services Development Centre, University of Stirling.

Aremyr, G. (1993) *Leve livet glemsk. Aktivisering av aldersdemente.* Oslo: Kommuneforlaget.

Athlin, E. and Norberg, A. (1987) 'Caregivers' Attitudes to and Interpretations of the Behavior of Severely Demented Patients During Feeding in a Patient Assignment Care System'. *International Journal of Nursing Studies 24,* 2, 145–153.

Axelsson, K., Norberg, A. and Asplund, K. (1984) 'En model för analys av et problem. Tillämpad på patienter med cerebrovasculär sjukdom på sjukhus.' *Socialmedicinsk tidsskrift 8/9.*

Berg, Grethe (1990) Uten mat og drikke: Måltidene som muligheter og utforinger i behandlingen av aldersdemente. *Info-banken rapport nr.3,* Tønsberg.

Blixen, K. (1975) *Skjebneanekdoter.* Oslo: Gyldendal.

Brækhus, A. (1999) 'Ikke-medikamentell behandling av lett demens.' *Tidsskrift for den Norske Lægeforening 27,* 4079–4082.

Bråne, G. (1988) 'Forandringer hos aldersdemente pasienter etter intervensjon i behandlingsmiljøet.' *Aldring og eldre 3.*

Bråne, G. (1997) *Att bedöma demens med GBS-skalan.* Stockholm: Natur och kultur.

Bull, G. and Magnus, J. (1996) *Omgivelser er terapi.* Sem: INFO-banken.

Burton-Jones, J. (1998) 'Sharing the Experience of Mealtimes in Homes.' *Journal of Dementia Care 13.* July–August.

Cohen, U. and Weismann, G.D. (1991) *Holding on to Home Designing Environments for People with Dementia.* Baltimore, MD: The John Hopkins University Press.

Davies, A.D.M. and Snaith, P.A. (1980) 'The social behavior of geriatric patients at mealtimes: An observational and intervention study'. *Age and Ageing 9*, 93–99.

Den Norske Stats Husbank (1998) *Omsorgsboliger og sykehjem. En veileder for lokalisering, organisering og utforming.* Oslo: Husbanken.

Dent, V. (2000) 'The Lunch Club 2000, Making Mealtimes Special.' *Journal of Dementia Care 3*, May–June.

Eek, A. and Nygård, Aa-M. (1999) *Innsyn og utsyn. Tilbud til personer med demens i norske kommuner.* Tønsberg/Oslo: Nasjonalt kompetansesenter for aldersdemens.

Ekman, S.L. and Norberg, A. (1988) 'The Autonomy of Demented Patients: Interviews with Care-givers.' *Journal of Medical Ethics 14*, 184-187.

Elwing, B. (1989) 'Mat för liv – mat för lust, hela livet ut.' *Socialmedicinsk Tidsskrift 7.*

Engedal, K. and Haugen, P.K. (1996) *Aldersdemens – Fakta og utfordringer.* Sem: INFO-banken.

Engedal, K., Kirkevold, Ø., Eek, A. and Nygård, Aa-M. (2000) *Rettighetsbegrensninger og bruk av tvangstiltak i behandling og omsorg av personer med demens.* Tønsberg/Oslo: Nasjonalt kompetansesenter for aldersdemens.

Hanserkers, J. (1987) *En värdig alderdom. Vård- och boendeformer för åldersdementa.* Lund: Studentlitteratur.

Haugen, P.K. (1981) *Aldersdemens og institusjonsmiljø. En litteraturgjennomgåelse av behandlingsmuligheter.* Norsk gerontologisk institutt, rapport nr 5.

Haugen, P.K., Eek, A., Kjeldsberg, A.-B. and Mordal, T. (1997) *OBS-demens – Et observasjonsskjema til bruk i miljøbehandling av eldre med mental svikt og demens. In 'Klippe, klippe...' sa kjerringa. Utvikling av behandlingstilbud til aldersdemente pasienter.* Sem: INFO-banken.

Heap, K. (1996) *Samtalen i eldreomsorgen.* Oslo: Kommuneforlaget.

Holthe, T. (1998) 'Hva anbefales for personer med demens?' *Ergoterapeuten 6*, 18–20.

Holthe, T., Kirkevold, Ø., Kjeldsberg, A.B. and Nygård, Aa-M. (eds) (1996) *Ti fugler på taket... Rapport fra konferanse om boliger for aldersdemente.* Sem: INFO-banken.

Judd, S., Marshall, M. and Phippen, P. (1998) 'Design for Dementia'. *The Journal of Dementia Care.* London: Hawker Publications Ltd.

Kittwood, T. (1999) *En revurdering av demens – personen kommer i første rekke.* Fredrikshavn: Dafolo forlag.

Kittwood, T. and Bredin K. (1992) *Person to Person: A Guide to the Care of Those with Failing Mental Powers.* Bradford: Bradford Dementia Group, University of Bradford.

Lillesveen, B. (1989) *Brumunddalsprosjektet.* Brumunddal: Brumunddal sykehjem, avd. for aldersdemente.

Lillesveen, B., Berg, G. and Skjerven, L. (1998) *Fra huggu tel næva'n.* Tønsberg/Oslo: Nasjonalt kompetansesenter for aldersdemens.

Lintern, T., Woods, B. and Phair, L. (2000) 'Training Is Not Enough to Change Care Practice'. *The Journal of Dementia Care 2,* 15–17.

Littlewood, S. and Saeidi, S. (1994) 'Therapeutic Mealtimes'. *Elderly Care 6,* 6, 20–21.

Malone, L. (1996) *Mealtimes and Dementia.* Scotland: Dementia Services Development Centre, University of Stirling.

Marshall, Mary (2003) *Food, Glorious Food – Perspectives on Food and Dementia.* London: Hawker Publications Ltd.

May, H. (1998) 'Striving for Competence can Undermine Well-being'. *Journal of Dementia Care 6,* 2.

Melin, L. and Götestam, G. (1981) 'The Effects of Rearranging Ward Routines on Communication and Eating Behaviors of Psychogeriatric Patients.' *Journal of Applied Behavior Analysis 14,* 47–51.

Munch, M. (1993) *Mot i brystet – vett i pannen.* Sem: INFO-banken.

Murphy, C.J. (1994) *'It Started with a Sea-shell', Life Story Work and People with Dementia.* Scotland: Dementia Services Development Centre, University of Stirling.

Noland, M. and Keady, J. (1996) 'Training Together: A Challenge for the Future.' *Journal of Dementia Care 5,* 10–13.

Notaker, Henry (1987) *Gastronomi – Til bords med historien.* Oslo: Aschehoug.

Nygård, Aa-M., Eek, A., Engedal, K. and Kirkvold, Ø. (1994) 'Ja, tenke det, ønske det, ville det med'. *Rapport fra Nasjonal konferanse om aldersdemens,* s. 99–108. Sem: INFO-banken.

Øvereng, A. (2000) 'Ettermiddagsuro'. *Demens 1,* 8–10.

Ramsby, Å. (1985) 'Goda resultat av gruppboende för senil dementa'. *Läkartidningen 82,* 38.

Raune, I. (1994) 'Större välbefinnande för en person med demens'. *Äldrecentrum 3,* s. 11–12.

Riis, B. (1986) *Aktiviseringsbehandling for aldersdemente. Et pilotprosjekt utført ved Ila servicehjem for eldre.* Oslo.

Riis, B. (1987) 'Aktivisering hever livskvaliteten hos aldersdemente'. *Fysioterapeuten 10,* 2–5.

Rokstad, A.M.M., Horn, B.L., Sarkstein, S. and Stendal, L.H. (1996) *Kommunikasjon på kollisjonskurs.* Sem: INFO-banken.

Sandman, P.O. and Norberg, A. (1988) 'Verbal Communication and Behavior During Meals in Five Institutionalized Patients with Alzheimer Type Dementia'. *Journal of Advanced Nursing 13,* 571–578.

Stortingsmelding nr. 28 (2000) *Innhald og kvalitet i omsorgstenestene.* Oslo: Det Kongelege Helse- og sosialdepartement.

Thorsen, K. (1993) 'Maten i livet.' In K.T. Elvbakken *Mat, alderdom og eldreomsorg.* Oslo: Kommuneforlaget.

Villemoes Sørensen, L. (1997) 'Demens giver aktivitetsproblemer'. *Ergoterapeuten 8.*

Wogn-Henriksen, K. (1997) *Siden blir det vel verre...?* Tønsberg/Oslo: Nasjonalt kompetansesenter for aldersdemens.